AF633305

Democracy for Winners Only: The Indian Paradox of Power, Participation, and Exclusion

OrangeBooks Publication

1st Floor, Rajhans Arcade, Mall Road, Kohka, Bhilai, Chhattisgarh 490020
Website: **www.orangebooks.in**

© Copyright, 2025, Author

All rights reserved. No part of this book may be reproduced, stored in a retrieval system, or transmitted, in any form by any means, electronic, mechanical, magnetic, optical, chemical, manual, photocopying, recording or otherwise, without the prior written consent of its writer.

First Edition, 2025

ISBN: 978-93-7426-136-1

Price: Rs. 200.00

The opinions/ contents expressed in this book are solely of the author and do not represent the opinions/ standings/ thoughts of OrangeBooks.

Printed in India

DEMOCRACY *for* WINNERS *Only*

THE INDIAN PARADOX OF POWER, PARTICIPATION, AND EXCLUSION

RAJ KUMAR SRIVASTAVA

OrangeBooks Publication
www.orangebooks.in

Dedication

To

Priyanka

Yash Shivani

Vaanchhita

Thank you for giving me carefree space to think, write and follow up my passion while filling my life with love laughter and quiet encouragement

Prologue
The Game of Democracy

When freedom becomes performance and equality becomes applause.

It began, as most Indian mornings do, with noise. The television blared election slogans, traffic horns competed with chants from a nearby rally, and on social media, victory memes flooded every feed. A country of 1.4 billion had once again chosen its winners. The anchors shouted "mandate," the newspapers declared "sweep," and the stock markets cheered. Amid the celebration, a quiet question rose: if everyone claims victory, who remembers the defeated or the unheard?

That question shaped this book.

For years, India's democracy has been measured by its size - the largest, the loudest, the longest. But scale is not the same as substance. Somewhere between ballot boxes and television debates, the soul of representation has thinned. Power has become a product, politics a marketplace, and participation a festival that ends by evening. We have built a democracy of performance - efficient, glittering, and fragile.

The idea for this book was born during my tenure as an Election Observer in the Sriperumbudur constituency of Tamil Nadu during the Lok Sabha elections of 2009. During my visit to a small polling booth in rural area I saw an elderly woman in a faded sari standing in line for hours to vote. When I asked why she waited so patiently, she smiled and said, "Because I can." Her simplicity carried the weight of generations who had once been denied that privilege. Yet later that day, in a city not far away, I met a young professional who shrugged, "My vote won't change anything." Between those two sentences — *because I can* and *it won't change anything*-lies the paradox of Indian democracy today.

This is not a book of cynicism. It is a book of contradictions - of faith and fatigue, freedom and exclusion, triumph and silence. It looks at democracy not through headlines but through human stories: a bureaucrat transferred for honesty, a journalist silenced by ownership, a migrant worker walking home invisible, a woman sarpanch learning to speak her own name at meetings. These are not isolated anecdotes; together, they form the pulse of the nation.

The title, *Democracy for Winners Only*, is not an accusation but an observation. Ours is a system that celebrates achievement yet mistrusts vulnerability. To lose an election is to vanish from discourse; to question authority is to risk identity. The Republic of Winners applauds ambition but forgets empathy. It believes that progress means pace, even when it leaves half the people behind. In such a culture, success becomes survival, and silence becomes policy.

Yet this same republic remains astonishingly resilient. Every few years, it surprises even its cynics. Voters change governments with the calm of routine; courts occasionally rediscover courage; activists rebuild communities brick by brick. For every failure of power, there is a whisper of conscience. The story of India is not a tragedy of democracy but its endless rehearsal.

This book moves across that landscape - from the glitter of power to the shadows of participation. It is written in three movements: **the making of winners**, **the mechanics of exclusion**, and **the rediscovery of equality**. The early chapters look at the machinery - elections, media, bureaucracy. The middle ones follow the people - the citizens who vote, protest, or vanish. The final ones search for what still binds us - ethics, equality, and empathy.

Each chapter combines reportage, reflection, and fragments of lived memory. The style is deliberate: to blend the moral urgency of journalism with the patience of storytelling. Because democracy, like literature, is not built on noise but on nuance.

I write as an observer, not a preacher - someone shaped by the bureaucracy and humbled by its contradictions. I have seen both the discipline of governance and the despair it hides. I have sat in offices where files decide destinies, and in villages where decisions arrive months late. The distance between the two is the space where democracy either breathes or breaks.

If there is a single argument that runs through these pages, it is this: **freedom alone does not sustain a republic - fairness does.** India has achieved liberty, but it is still negotiating equality. That negotiation happens daily - in ration lines, classrooms, WhatsApp groups, and courtrooms. The republic is not one grand structure; it is a million small acts of decency.

The coming decades will test us in ways our founders could never have imagined. Artificial intelligence will replace jobs faster than education can create them. Climate change will redraw maps faster than policies can adapt. Inequality will deepen even as connectivity expands. In that uncertainty, the question will return: who is the republic for?

Perhaps the answer lies not in policy but in practice - in the way we treat those who lose, those who disagree, those who remain unseen. Because democracy, at its purest, is not about who rules the nation but about who belongs to it.

So this book begins with a salute - not to the victors on television screens, but to the millions who keep showing up: to vote, to teach, to write, to clean, to heal, to argue. They are the republic's quiet founders, renewing it without ceremony.

If freedom was our first victory, equality must be our next.

And maybe, when we finally learn to share victory, we will no longer need to measure democracy by who wins.

Table of Contents

Chapter – 1
The Republic of Winners

Freedom gave us equality of opportunity; competition replaced it with hierarchy of result.

At half past nine on counting day, the newsroom of a national TV channel erupted as the election ticker crossed three hundred seats for the ruling alliance. Anchors stood on tables waving miniature flags. Producers clapped like cricket fans. In a small tea stall opposite the building, a delivery boy watched the same screen through a cracked window. The ticker had climbed, the prices in his city had too. He shrugged and went back to washing glasses. The celebration of democracy had never felt so far from the people who sustained it.

India's democracy calls itself the world's largest festival of choice, yet the sound of victory now drowns out the whisper of participation. In 2019, the capital's boulevards were decked with saffron bunting. Loudspeakers blared slogans that merged faith with triumph. Meanwhile, in drought-stricken Marathwada, villagers gathered under a tamarind tree to discuss which candidate might at least visit once in five years. "We vote for water, they count votes for power," said Rukmini, a farm widow who had lost her husband to debt two monsoons earlier. Her sentence captured the arithmetic of this republic: the more invisible your life, the louder the rhetoric of your representation.

The Republic of Winners is not a metaphor — it is an economy of attention. Every institution, from Parliament to panchayat, is graded by how visibly it succeeds. When a collector in Madhya Pradesh painted school walls blue and won an award, newspapers called her "the model officer." When another collector refused illegal mining leases and was transferred, no one wrote his name. Bureaucracy, like politics, has learnt to pose for photographs. A file moves faster when a camera waits outside the room.

During the 2024 campaign, drones filmed rallies that resembled rock concerts. Slogans were tested like jingles. Advertising agencies coined taglines; influencers were hired to humanize leaders. In a booth near Varanasi, volunteers handed out QR-coded pamphlets promising digital jobs and solar subsidies. The villagers scanned the codes only to find links to speeches. "It's like online shopping," one farmer joked. "You add promises to the cart; delivery never comes."

Media turned the process into a morality play. Channels divided the nation into two colours: one for patriots, another for pessimists. When opposition candidates protested the misuse of investigative agencies, they were asked if they "accepted the people's verdict." In this televised republic, the victor embodies the people; the defeated represent only themselves. Debates became duels, and news anchors became generals leading armies of hashtags.

The contagion of competition spread beyond politics. In Delhi's Rajender Nagar , thousands of UPSC aspirants fill hostels each June, memorizing essays on ethics and governance. They call it "the exam of destiny." Outside one coaching centre, a hoarding displays portraits of last year's toppers. Under each smiling face is the word *winner*. For the ones who failed by a few marks, there is only silence. A sociology teacher there confided, "We've made success look moral, and failure immoral." The same disease afflicts democracy itself.

Economy amplifies this moral divide. In Surat's diamond district, traders boast of record exports and growth. Two hundred kilometres away, in Dahod, tribal women sell forest produce for coins that haven't changed value in twenty years. "GDP grows in cities; hunger stays in forests," said a local activist during a 2023 livelihood survey. Yet every budget speech begins with the phrase "the nation's growth story." Growth for whom becomes a question too impolite to ask.

The myth of meritocracy sustains the illusion. When billionaires appear on magazine covers as "self-made," the republic applauds without asking who built their roads or whose subsidies underwrite their success. In Noida, a start-up founder who secured a government innovation grant confessed privately that most awards go to those already networked. "Connections are the new credentials," he said. Merit is merely privilege made polite.

The Republic of Winners also thrives on forgetfulness. Each tragedy becomes yesterday's trending topic. When migrants walked hundreds of kilometres during the 2020 lockdown, television cameras filmed their blistered feet; by 2021, the same channels hailed "vaccine victory." The State learnt that endurance has no constituency. By the next election, the migrants had vanished from memory and manifestos alike.

Yet resistance flickers at the margins. In a dusty lane of Bhilai, a group of contract workers gather every evening after their shifts. They call themselves the *People's Parliament*. There is no dais, no gavel - just a bench and a battered diary where grievances are recorded. When asked why they bother, one of them replied, "Because if we stop talking, they'll think we agree." In that sentence lies democracy's last defense — conversation.

India's founding generation imagined power as stewardship, not spectacle. Ambedkar warned that political democracy without social democracy is a "house built on sand." Seventy-five years later, that house gleams with LED lights but trembles under inequity. From the selfie walls of government schemes to the trending hashtags of nationalism, the republic rewards visibility, not virtue.

Late one night, in a small village near Prayagraj, an old man who had voted in every election since 1952 was asked whom he would choose this time. He smiled and said, “I vote for hope each time; I lose every time; still, I go.” His wrinkled thumb, still inked, was the truest mark of citizenship — not victory, but endurance. The Republic of Winners will endure too, but only if it remembers that democracy’s finest hour is not when someone wins, but when everyone is allowed to lose with dignity.

Chapter – 2
Losers by Design

How caste, class, and gender decide who loses before the contest begins.

In July 2023, when Bihar released its long-awaited caste survey, Patna's streets briefly turned into a seminar. Rickshaw-pullers quoted percentages; college professors argued about sub-quotas in tea stalls. The numbers told an old truth in new language: more than half the population belonged to communities owning less than one percent of land. Democracy had equal ballots but unequal beginnings. *"Hamare vote barabar hain, zindagi nahi,"* murmured a vegetable vendor near Kankarbagh market - our votes are equal, our lives are not. His sentence summarized a nation where defeat is embedded in design.

Travel east to a panchayat in Araria district. Under a mango tree, forty-year-old Sangeeta Devi signs attendance at the MGNREGA muster roll. Her thumbprint glistens in purple ink. Officially she is a “beneficiary,” one among millions who make India’s social-security statistics look impressive. But when she asks the block officer about delayed wages, he shrugs: “System error.” The digital platform that advertises transparency has no button for urgency. Sangeeta’s poverty funds the efficiency of others.

Caste remains the most persistent architect of losing. In Bundelkhand, every election poster still carries subtle cues: a red tilak here, a surname there, a whisper of belonging. In 2022, a Dalit candidate in Banda filed nomination papers with borrowed money and borrowed hope. His wife pawned her wedding chain to pay the deposit. He lost by fifty thousand votes and a lifetime of credibility. “People said they liked my ideas,” he said later, “but they didn’t want to waste their vote.” Merit dies quietly under the tyranny of arithmetic.

The middle class, which prides itself on merit, seldom notices how much subsidy lubricates its success — tax concessions on housing, cheap fuel for scooters, English-medium schooling inherited rather than earned. In the alleys of Mukherjee Nagar, aspirants study for the civil-service exam, convinced that hard work alone will rescue them. But each coaching batch costs nearly ₹1.5 lakh. For the son of a daily-wage mason in Gaya, that is two years of income. He studies anyway, in a room without a fan, repeating motivational quotes printed on glossy coaching posters. The system keeps him dreaming because dreaming is cheaper than reform.

Gender adds another layer to this engineered inequality. In Rajasthan's Barmer district, 2024's local-body elections saw women winning a record number of seats - on paper. Most are "*proxy sarpanches,*" their husbands signing documents behind curtains. One of them, Kamla Bai, laughed when asked why she let her husband run the office. "He can read English," she said simply. Education, not law, decides power. Yet in Kerala's Kudumbashree cooperatives, another possibility flickers: women's groups controlling microcredit, planting vegetable gardens, even deciding panchayat budgets. Where the system loosens its hierarchy, equality starts to look practical, not poetic.

The urban–rural chasm widens every season. In Gurgaon's glass towers, start-ups raise millions on the promise of "disrupting inequality." A few kilometres away, in Nathupur village, domestic workers clean those towers and return to homes where the drains overflow during monsoon. Their Aadhaar cards proclaim them citizens of the same republic, but citizenship now measures bandwidth. When electricity fails, the elevator stalls — a metaphor for social mobility in India: glamorous until the power cuts.

Economic design compounds social design. Electoral politics runs on money that flows upstream. In 2019, the Association for Democratic Reforms found that 88 percent of MPs were crorepatis. Contesting a parliamentary seat can cost more than ₹7 crore. Political parties deny tickets to the poor because "winnability" correlates with wealth. It is democracy outsourced to finance. The small independent candidate, once a village hero, now sells his candidacy to a bigger party in exchange for survival. The market has replaced ideology with franchise.

Consider the 2020 migrant-worker exodus. When trains stopped and highways filled with barefoot families, the nation glimpsed its invisible majority. Men pushing children in steel carts through May heat, women carrying sacks and infants together — these were not victims of a sudden lockdown but of a long neglect. Their march was not merely from city to village; it was from promise to memory. The republic watched them on screens, posted hashtags, and moved on. The losers of policy became the scenery of empathy.

Education was meant to be the ladder out. Yet the ladder stands on uneven ground. In a government school in Dantewada, a teacher uses a single smartphone to show videos to sixty Adivasi children. The 5G India on posters ends where the forest begins. Meanwhile, an ed-tech company in Bengaluru sells "affordable learning plans" for ₹30 000 a year — a bargain only for those who never worry about rations. Knowledge has become a subscription service.

The bureaucracy that should balance inequality often replicates it. "Parliamentary data indicate that there have been around 11,000 IAS officers between 1951 and 2020, with only about one in ten being women. Detailed, public, all-India figures for SC/ST representation across the entire period are still hard to obtain, but available recruitment data suggest that ST representation has remained in low. When an ST officer in Chhattisgarh refused to clear a questionable mining lease, he was transferred to a remote posting within a week. "I thought I joined to serve the people," he said, "but the file serves whoever signs it last." Integrity, like poverty, is punished for being inconvenient.

Religious and regional identities, too, are recalibrated into hierarchies of legitimacy. In Manipur's hills, Kuki villages burnt while officials debated jurisdiction. In the plains, Meitei civil groups held victory rallies. Both claimed to defend democracy; neither saw its collapse in their own reflection. The State's silence measured whose suffering counted.

And yet, even in this architecture of exclusion, small rebellions persist. In Odisha's Kandhamal, a group of Dalit and tribal women formed a forest cooperative after losing their husbands to cyclone Fani. They plant bamboo, sell baskets, and refuse to take middlemen's advances. "They used to call us helpless widows," said their leader Pratima Nayak. "Now they call us competitors." The word tastes better on her tongue than any welfare scheme could provide.

In 2021, farmers camping on Delhi's borders taught the nation the grammar of patience. They faced tear gas, barricades, and months of winter. When the laws were finally repealed, they didn't declare victory; they said, "We were heard." In that statement lies a moral inversion of the Republic of Winners. For those designed to lose, being heard is itself a triumph.

The persistence of losers keeps democracy alive. It forces the system to rehearse its ideals even when it forgets them. Every protestor, every student demanding fairness in exams, every whistle-blower resisting transfers — they are the republic's moral infrastructure. Their defeats remind India what success was supposed to mean.

At dusk in a Bihar village, Sangeeta Devi finishes her day at the worksite and walks home past election posters fading in the rain. She doesn't remember the candidate's promises, only that he once came in an air-conditioned car. She will vote again next time, not because she expects to win, but because not voting would confirm her defeat. Democracy survives in that thin margin between resignation and faith — a space the winners seldom visit but the losers keep clean.

Chapter – 3
The Mathematics of Power

When 37% of votes become 100% of power.

On counting day in 2019, a young teacher in Aligarh sat before his television with a notebook. Each tick on the screen meant one more seat for the party he opposed. By noon, he closed the notebook, saying softly, “They’ve already won on WhatsApp.” His remark wasn’t cynical—it was mathematical. India’s democracy, once measured by ideals, now thrives on calculation.

In India’s First-Past-the-Post system, victory doesn’t require majority consensus, only efficient distribution. The 2019 general election handed one party 303 seats with just 37 percent of the national vote. In Goa in 2017, Congress secured more seats but the BJP formed the government through post-election arithmetic. In Tripura’s 2023 assembly polls, a three-way contest allowed a party with barely one-third of the votes to claim total power. Arithmetic, it seems, has replaced argument as the soul of politics.

The design was meant to simplify democracy; instead, it has turned representation into a gamble. A 2 percent swing in vote share can flip entire states. In Uttar Pradesh, micro-targeting of caste groups now determines cabinet portfolios. Electoral strategists speak of "vote-bank clusters" the way bankers speak of assets. "We can predict results in 60 percent of constituencies just from last week's booth-level data," said a political consultant in Lucknow, tapping on his iPad during the 2024 campaign. "The rest is noise." But that noise is the sound of millions whose preferences fall outside the formula.

Arithmetic creates an illusion of stability even when society fragments. In 2020, Delhi re-elected its local government by an overwhelming margin, but within a month, communal riots ripped through its neighborhoods. Electoral victory had masked moral collapse. Numbers reassured the rulers even as fires burned in their capital.

The obsession with majority has deformed governance itself. Bureaucrats speak of "deliverables" and "targets," borrowing the language of project management. When a state launches 100-day programs, it measures output in kilometers of road, not the lives reshaped along it. During the "Swachh Bharat Mission", villages rushed to build toilets to meet deadlines; by 2021, a Comptroller and Auditor General report showed thousands of them lacked water connections. But on dashboards, the figures glowed green — achievement unlocked.

The electoral system's bias toward concentration discourages coalition and punishes nuance. The result is a winner-takes-all psychology. Opposition parties, cornered by scale, mimic the ruling party's methods rather than challenge its logic. Manifestos shrink into slogan cards; rallies turn into theatre. In Tamil Nadu, 2024's campaign jingles were composed by film studios; in Rajasthan, candidates rented LED vans streaming promises like commercials. "We run elections like product launches now," a campaign manager admitted. "The one with more reach wins, even if the product fails."

Money, the second arithmetic of power, completes the loop. Electoral Bonds — the anonymous donation instrument introduced in 2018 — have channeled more than ₹16,000 crore into party coffers, a huge percent to the ruling side. Each bond buys not just influence but invisibility. When the Supreme Court finally struck down the scheme in 2024, few donors came forward. They didn't need to - the returns were already delivered through contracts, posts, and silence. Political investment had become safer than stock markets.

Technology sharpened the math. In 2024, volunteers in Madhya Pradesh used AI tools to simulate how local caste combinations might vote. Software called *Pratibimb* calculated "winning margins" based on social-media sentiment and historical data. Booth captains were trained not in persuasion but in precision.

"We know which families shift last-minute," one told me. "We don't need speeches; we need WhatsApp reminders." Representation had become a predictive model.

Yet in Kerala's Wayanad, a different experiment in counting continues. Each panchayat meeting begins with the reading of household data — not to exclude, but to ensure inclusion. When citizens themselves verify beneficiary lists, corruption dips and dignity rises. There, arithmetic serves empathy. "We use numbers to listen," said an old woman in the Puthuppadi Gram Sabha. "In Delhi, they use numbers to speak."

The fixation on percentages has infected media too. On every result day, anchors perform arithmetic gymnastics: vote shares, strike rates, swing margins. In 2024, one channel introduced a "Democracy Dashboard" that looked like a stock exchange — seats up, alliances down. The citizen becomes a spectator of numbers, not a participant in governance. "We are counting democracy to death," a retired editor sighed.

Even policy debates are hostage to quantification. Governments tout the number of toilets built, start-ups registered, or kilometers electrified. Missing are measures of well-being: hunger, dignity, learning. When an economy grows by eight percent but child malnutrition persists at 35 percent, the arithmetic of success hides a moral deficit. The poor contribute labour to the numerator but live in the denominator.

Representation, once a moral bond, has turned transactional. The voter is valued only in aggregates. A villager in Dantewada put it bluntly: “They count us before the election, not after.” In Kashmir, the delimitation exercise redrew boundaries to “balance representation,” yet locals whispered that arithmetic had replaced autonomy. “They moved the lines so we could be counted differently,” said a shopkeeper in Anantnag. Democracy’s map had been redrawn by geometry, not justice.

But arithmetic also produces ironies. In Maharashtra’s 2022 political crisis, two factions of the same party claimed the mandate. Courts cited numbers; citizens saw betrayal. “It’s like a cricket match,” quipped a farmer from Nashik. “Whoever has the umpire wins.” His humour hid exhaustion. For the ordinary voter, each recalculation feels like subtraction.

Still, the language of counting can be reclaimed. In Rajasthan’s social audits, citizens confront contractors with expenditure sheets. In Jharkhand’s forest-rights hearings, villagers tally land parcels reclaimed from illegal leases. Their mathematics is moral - proof that numbers can hold power accountable instead of excusing it.

The tragedy of Indian democracy is not that it miscounts votes, but that it stops counting lives once votes are counted. A retired bureaucrat in Bengaluru recalled his training days in the 1970s. “We were taught to serve the last person in the queue,” he said. “Now we only count how many are left in line.” His lament defines the republic’s new arithmetic: progress tallied, justice deferred.

Late one night after the 2024 election results, the same teacher from Aligarh reopened his notebook. On the first page, he drew two columns - votes won, votes lost - and then added a third: *voices unheard.* "This is the real majority," he whispered. Outside, the city burst into fireworks. The television announced another landslide. Inside, a single citizen did his own counting - one that democracy still refuses to learn.

Chapter – 4
Politics as Business, Citizens as Consumers

The marketization of governance and the price of participation.

In a crowded chowk in Hyderabad during the 2024 election campaign, two teenagers debated political choices with the same tone they used to compare mobile phones. "This party gives more benefits," said one. "Yes," the other replied, "but the other has better branding." Their laughter carried the truth of modern democracy: the voter is no longer a citizen deliberating on policy, but a consumer comparing offers.

Politics has become India's largest marketplace. Parties now advertise schemes like consumer products, complete with launch events, logos, and jingles. When Tamil Nadu's "Amma canteens" or Delhi's "Mohalla

Clinics" appeared on billboards, the idea was less welfare, more recall value. Voters are courted through campaigns designed by marketing agencies that once sold soaps and cars. During the 2024 elections, candidates hired "influencer managers" to craft Instagram reels. The line between policy and promotion blurred; governance became an exercise in packaging.

The Election Commission's expenditure reports show that political advertising in 2024 crossed ₹8,000 crores - more than the entire rural employment budget of some states. Drone shows, holographic rallies, and AI-generated campaign videos turned politics into theatre. "Every speech has to trend by evening," explained a digital strategist in Bengaluru. "If it doesn't, it's as if it never happened." Democracy was now an algorithm, constantly refreshed for engagement.

In Andhra Pradesh, where welfare has become the lingua franca of politics, an old woman at a polling booth in Anantapur summed up the new ethos. "I don't care who wins," she said, "as long as my pension arrives on time." Her pragmatism is not cynicism—it's survival. Successive governments have turned welfare into brand identity: YSR pensions, Amma meals, Modi Awas. The beneficiary becomes a loyal customer. Gratitude replaces rights; dependency replaces accountability.

Every subsidy now carries a photograph. LPG cylinders under the Ujjwala Yojana bear the Prime Minister's face; free power bills in Telangana are embossed with the Chief Minister's signature. When benefits are personalised, the state recedes into the shadow of personality. “I am giving you,” says the leader, erasing the idea that citizens fund their own welfare through taxes. The voter learns to thank, not question.

At a ration shop in Odisha’s Mayurbhanj district, the shopkeeper keeps a laminated poster of the local MLA beside the price list. “He got us this ration card,” he says. When asked if he means the law or the leader, he smiles, unsure of the difference. The confusion is deliberate: democracy thrives on the illusion of direct generosity, even when it’s funded by collective revenue.

The cost of this illusion is staggering. The average expense of winning a Lok Sabha seat in 2024 exceeded ₹12 crore, nearly twice that of 2019. Candidates mortgage properties, take loans, or rely on corporate patrons. For many, politics is an investment portfolio—losses in one constituency are offset by contracts, tenders, or governorships later. A defeated candidate in Madhya Pradesh explained it bluntly: “I lost the election, not the access.”

Money flows both ways. In return for donations, corporations expect favorable policies or regulatory silence. After the 2024 Supreme Court verdict exposing major donors under the Electoral Bonds scheme, one CEO privately admitted, “We paid all sides. Democracy is our insurance policy.” The Republic of Winners, it seems, also has shareholders.

Bureaucracy mirrors this corporate culture. Officers are rated by their ability to “deliver results” rather than ensure fairness. A collector in Gujarat who posted weekly project updates on Twitter was hailed as a "digital hero," while another who refused a politically pressured land transfer was sidelined. "Governance has become optics management," said a senior IAS officer. "We have dashboards for everything except ethics."

The commodification of governance extends to crisis. During the 2020 pandemic, state governments competed for credit over oxygen supplies. Relief funds carried brand labels; chief ministers printed their faces on vaccination certificates. Even grief became a public-relations exercise. When a journalist questioned the accuracy of death data in Gujarat, a ruling party spokesperson replied, "Why focus on negativity?" In a consumer democracy, bad news is bad branding.

Meanwhile, citizens have internalized market logic. The phrase "return on vote" circulates casually in rural conversations. In Maharashtra's Sangli district, a group of sugarcane farmers compared MSP promises the way traders compare stock prices. "We'll sell our votes to whoever offers the best rate," one said without irony. The moral language of citizenship has been replaced by the transactional dialect of the bazaar.

Technology has deepened this transformation. Digital campaigns micro-target citizens based on caste, income, and location. In 2024, a political app called *JanConnect* claimed to reach fifty million voters through "personalized governance messaging." The app sent daily updates thanking users for their "support in nation-building." For rural youth, it was the first time politics addressed them directly-but also the first time their data was mined in return. The algorithm became the new manifesto.

The privatization of politics mirrors the privatization of everything else. Ministries outsource communications to PR firms, and government schemes are designed with logo guidelines like commercial products. In Delhi, one advertising agency handles campaigns for both a major political party and several government departments. "It's the same client, really," a creative director admitted, "just a different brief."

Even dissent is marketed now. NGOs must brand their causes to attract donors. Environmental groups talk in hashtags; farmer unions design merchandise. The performance of resistance risks becoming indistinguishable from the performance of power. A young activist in Jharkhand sighed, "If your protest isn't livestreamed, it doesn't exist." The struggle for justice must now compete with entertainment for attention.

Yet amidst this glittering marketplace, faint acts of defiance persist. In 2023, when ASHA workers in Kerala marched to demand minimum wages, they carried hand-painted banners reading, "We are not beneficiaries; we are citizens." Their slogan didn't trend but their strike succeeded after ten days. In that moment, democracy looked less like a product and more like a process — messy, slow, but human.

A tea-seller near Mysuru offered another parable. "Leaders promise like shopkeepers," he said. "We customers know half their goods are fake, but we buy anyway, because the next shop sells the same." His laughter was weary but wise. Politics as business can sell hope, but it cannot deliver trust.

When the lights dim after election rallies, only the unglamorous work of governance remains: repairing potholes, paying teachers, stocking health centers. But those who treat politics as business rarely stay for maintenance; they move on to the next campaign. The citizen, reduced to consumer, is left holding the receipt.

India's democracy began as a moral experiment - an attempt to turn equality into everyday behavior. It now risks becoming a retail ecosystem of promises. But the story isn't over. In quiet corners of the country, where social audits confront corruption and women's self-help groups demand accountability, the old idea of citizenship still breathes. It doesn't need billboards or hashtags. It needs listening, and the courage to ask, not just receive.

Chapter – 5
The Bureaucracy of Winners

How performance optics replace moral purpose in public service.

In 2014, a young IAS officer in Uttar Pradesh stood before a district collectorate full of cameras. She had just seized several illegal sand-mining trucks owned by a politically connected contractor. By evening, she was transferred. The news cycle celebrated her for 48 hours and forgot her by the weekend. “I followed the law,” she said later. “They followed the system.” Her story, like hundreds of others across India, reveals how governance has transformed from public service into performance - and the bureaucracy has become its most reluctant actor.

India’s bureaucracy was conceived as the invisible machine of democracy, quietly turning files and implementing policy beyond political passions. But today's administrative culture runs on optics. Every officer is expected to perform success - measurable, photogenic, and social-media ready. At district offices across India, dashboards blink like stock tickers: toilets built, trees planted, grievances resolved. What cannot be measured might as well not exist.

In Madhya Pradesh, a collector boasts that his district is "100 percent ODF," though local villagers confess they still use fields. "If I report failure," he admits, "I become the failure." The chain of accountability runs upward, not outward. The government measures compliance, not conviction. A retired secretary in Delhi describes it as "a performance economy of governance." Under pressure to show progress, bureaucrats learn to equate success with visibility.

The bureaucratic version of the "winner's curse" manifests as constant transfer and quiet submission. According to the Indian Administrative Service Association's 2022 data, an average IAS officer is transferred every 16 months. In some states, that number drops to less than a year. "It's hard to build anything lasting when you live out of cartons," says a district magistrate in Odisha. "You stop taking stands; you take precautions."

Transfers have become the currency of obedience. During the pandemic, officers who questioned inflated death data were moved to "non-field" postings. One health officer in Gujarat recalls how he tried to report oxygen shortages in May 2021. "They told me to manage the narrative, not the patients," he said quietly.

The bureaucrat's tragedy lies in the shrinking space between conscience and career.

Technology, initially hailed as a weapon against corruption, has produced a subtler tyranny - of constant surveillance. Every file in the new e-office system can be tracked, timestamped, and graded. "Earlier, we feared politicians; now we fear algorithms," says a young officer in Jharkhand. Efficiency is the new morality. The danger is that governance becomes mechanical - fast but soulless, transparent but indifferent.

The rise of the "celebrity officer" reflects this change. Some collectors now have more social-media followers than local MLAs. Instagram reels show them planting saplings, inspecting schools, or scolding negligent staff - all under soft filters and heroic captions. While many are genuinely dedicated, the system rewards virality over virtue. "If you want funding, trend first," jokes a deputy collector in Maharashtra. Governance has become content creation.

Yet beneath these glamorous narratives, the ground staff-revenue clerks, panchayat secretaries, ASHA workers - struggle with chronic delays in pay and impossible workloads. In 2023, ASHA unions in Haryana protested for weeks demanding minimum wages. "They call us frontline warriors, but we can't afford medicine," one worker said. The bureaucracy's pyramid of prestige ensures that the closer you are to the people, the smaller your reward.

Corruption, though more sophisticated, hasn't disappeared - it has digitized. In Bihar's rural works department, tender approvals are routed through online portals that mask manual manipulation. "Everything is paperless now," an insider explains, "including accountability." Kickbacks are coded into consultancy fees and third-party audits. The ghost of red tape has been reborn as a spreadsheet.

Meanwhile, officers who resist the tide often face institutional gas lighting. In 2022, a forest officer in Chhattisgarh who refused to clear tree felling for a coal project was labelled "anti-development." His note citing environmental violations was quietly deleted from the final file. "They call me emotional," he said. "As if empathy were unprofessional." The bureaucracy's moral vocabulary no longer includes empathy; it only recognizes efficiency.

To understand this shift, walk into any collector's office. The decor tells the story: motivational posters, LED dashboards, and a glass wall separating visitors from staff. Citizens wait outside clutching petitions, while inside, meetings unfold in PowerPoint. "People come here to see progress," says one officer. "Not to participate in it." The administration, once a bridge, has become a showcase.

The irony is that many officers join the civil service with idealism intact. The training academies in Mussoorie and Hyderabad still echo with oaths to uphold the Constitution. But once in the field, they learn another Constitution - unwritten, practical, and enforced by survival. The unwritten Article 1 reads: "The government is always right."

Yet amid this moral erosion, flickers of integrity persist. In Kerala, a district collector who made Gram Sabhas mandatory before approving new development projects faced initial ridicule but later praise when his model improved transparency. In Mizoram, officials partnered with churches to run vaccination drives during the pandemic, achieving near-universal coverage without coercion. These stories prove that the system's soul is dormant, not dead.

The bureaucracy's complicity in India's inequality is not born of malice but of fatigue. Officers juggle files that affect millions, but they rarely see the faces behind the figures. A block development officer in Jharkhand confided, "We handle poverty in Excel sheets; after a while, the poor become data points." The detachment is a defense mechanism, a way to survive moral exhaustion.

The "Republic of Winners" demands administrative cheerleaders, not custodians. But democracy requires the opposite - institutions that question, slow down, and sometimes refuse. Every reform - from RTI to the Forest Rights Act - was won because a bureaucrat somewhere decided to interpret law as justice, not convenience.

In 2024, during an internal review meeting in Delhi, a senior officer remarked, "We must build a 21st-century bureaucracy." Another voice from the back added, "We must first build a 19th-century conscience." The laughter was uneasy because the truth was near.

A few weeks later, I met the young officer who had been transferred for stopping illegal mining a decade earlier. She now works in education. "I've learnt not to fight every battle," she said, "but not to forget why I joined." Behind her desk hung a framed quote by Rabindranath Tagore: *"Power said to the world, you are mine; the world kept it prisoner. Love said, I am yours; the world gave itself."*

The bureaucracy will reclaim its dignity only when it rediscovers love - love for law, for people, for principle. Until then, it will remain a republic of administrators managing appearances. Democracy may survive without idealism, but it cannot thrive without conscience. And conscience, like freedom, begins with one person refusing to obey injustice quietly.

Chapter – 6
Media, Myth and Manufactured Winners

When visibility becomes validity and news becomes narrative.

In the newsroom of a leading Hindi channel on election night 2024, a producer shouted, “Bigger graphics! More drums!” The anchor, drenched in sweat and spotlight, rehearsed his war cry: “This is not just an election - it’s a revolution!” The newsroom floor looked less like a place of journalism and more like a film set. In the corner, a young intern whispered, “We already know the result; we just need better visuals.” That whisper captured what Indian media has become - a theatre of triumphs, where the story of democracy is told through the grammar of mythmaking.

Television was once the conscience of the Republic. In the 1990s, *The World This Week* narrated facts with restraint, and Doordarshan debates carried civility. By the 2010s, a new lexicon had arrived: "breaking," "exclusive," "first on our channel." By 2024, even "truth" had an aesthetic -delivered with fireworks, applause, and computer-generated maps. The news was no longer to inform, but to perform.

The collapse of credibility began slowly. In 2016, a journalist in Chhattisgarh reporting on illegal mining received threats; his editor replaced him with someone "more manageable." In 2022, a veteran reporter in Lucknow was suspended for questioning a government data release. The message to journalists was clear: silence travels faster than truth. "We are not asked to lie," one senior anchor confided, "just to not tell the whole story."

The fusion of media and power was cemented by ownership. By 2022, more than 80 percent of Indian news channels were controlled by corporate groups with direct political links. When NDTV, one of the few independent voices, was acquired by a conglomerate in 2022, it was described as a "business decision." But journalists understood it as a message: dissent had been bought out. "You can't fight power when it's also your advertiser," a producer said. The line between newsroom and boardroom dissolved into a common pursuit - profit through propaganda.

Social media accelerated the decay. Twitter (now X) and WhatsApp became the new frontlines. The Information and Broadcasting Ministry's "fact-check unit" routinely flagged satire as misinformation while ignoring coordinated hate campaigns. In 2023, a viral deepfake of a woman journalist criticizing the government circulated on thousands of phones before fact-checkers caught up. "By then," she said, "my parents had stopped talking to me." Lies travelled faster than apologies, and apologies rarely aired at prime time.

Anchors began to perform patriotism like theatre. In one viral moment, a news host wrapped himself in the tricolor to denounce "anti-national elements." Another broadcast an entire show standing on a model tank. Every debate became a war, every critic a traitor. The camera panned from outrage to advertisement without pause. Between commercials for cement and smartphones, the anchors sold certainty. The viewer, exhausted but addicted, surrendered to the spectacle. "We don't watch news to know anymore," said a shopkeeper in Kanpur. "We watch to feel."

Election coverage completed the transformation. In 2024, exit polls were packaged like cricket matches. Anchors yelled "strike rate," "run rate," and "boundary seats." When one opposition party gained marginally, a rival channel labelled it "moral corruption." Objectivity, once a profession's pride, was now a liability. "I had to quit," said a young journalist from Pune. "I joined to ask questions, not to chant slogans."

Regional media, once a refuge of authenticity, faces its own crisis. Small-town reporters survive on "stringer payments" - ₹300 per story, no job security. Many double as advertising agents or party workers. In Jharkhand, a journalist who exposed corruption in the district administration was booked under defamation laws. "They say I'm anti-development," he laughed bitterly. "I just asked why the road disappeared after the photo-op."

In the digital age, propaganda has become participatory. Every citizen is a broadcaster. During the 2023 Manipur conflict, manipulated videos spread faster than relief messages, inflaming hate. Tech-savvy trolls, organized into "IT cells," flooded social media with doctored clips. Algorithms reward emotion, not verification. "Outrage is free fuel," said a digital strategist. "People share what they fear." Democracy, once a conversation, has become a chain reaction.

Behind the noise, the economics of silence thrives. Government advertising budgets have grown fivefold since 2014, distributed selectively. Channels that toe the line receive campaigns; critics receive audits. A journalist in Delhi's press club joked, "Freedom of press is alive - but on a ventilator owned by the state." When the Press Council of India occasionally protests, it is ignored as politely as a traffic signal at midnight.

Not all hope is lost. In 2024, a small independent newsroom in Kerala, *The Fourth Estate*, exposed irregularities in land deals involving powerful politicians. The story went viral online before mainstream outlets could bury it. In Telangana, community radio stations continue to air farmers' grievances in local dialects, resisting the glamour of national noise. These small bastions of integrity remind us that journalism's purpose is not to amplify power but to interrogate it.

The myth of the media as a "fourth pillar" has collapsed because the first three - legislature, executive, and judiciary - have learned to lean on it rather than be watched by it. When cameras follow leaders instead of citizens, democracy becomes choreography. The press conferences are choreographed; questions are pre-approved. A veteran political correspondent recalls the difference: "In the 1990s, we chased politicians; now they chase us - to hand us talking points."

Still, truth finds unconventional routes. During the pandemic, citizen journalists livestreamed hospital shortages, forcing authorities to act. In 2021, when a crematorium worker in Ghaziabad uploaded photos of mass pyres, he was threatened with dismissal but saved countless lives by exposing neglect. Truth, like water, finds cracks.

The republic's media doesn't need more technology; it needs more courage. The journalist's job is not to entertain, but to endure. In an age of information abundance, silence is complicity. The ordinary viewer, too, must learn to doubt - to question every headline that confirms comfort. "Misinformation thrives because it flatters," said a professor of journalism in Chennai. "We believe what makes us feel right." Democracy, by contrast, demands the humility to be wrong.

In the quiet of a rural newsroom in Nagaland, a young reporter named Temjen sits before a borrowed laptop. His paper, printed weekly, carries stories of disappearing forests and unpaid teachers. "We don't go viral," he says with a smile, "but we reach people." The hum of his printer competes with the roar of televised shouting thousands of kilometers away. Somewhere between those sounds lies India's real conversation -fragile, human, unfinished.

If the Republic of Winners is powered by applause, then journalism must rediscover the courage of listening. For truth doesn't need volume; it needs patience. And in a land where even silence can be weaponized, perhaps the bravest act left is to speak softly, and persist.

Chapter – 7
The Psychology of Defeat

What happens when losing becomes synonymous with disloyalty.

On a humid afternoon in March 1977, Indira Gandhi stood before cameras outside her residence, smiling faintly as she conceded defeat. The nation had just ended the Emergency with a single vote. Her tone was calm, almost maternal: *"The people have spoken; we accept the verdict."* That moment, brief and unscripted, remains one of the most graceful acts in Indian politics. Forty-seven years later, defeat has lost its dignity.

Today, losing is treated like contamination. On television, a defeated candidate is asked not about lessons but about "damage control." Party spokespersons rehearse excuses - EVM malfunction, fake news, vote splitting. The word *mandate* has turned sacred only for winners. In India's new political psychology, to lose is not to disagree; it is to disappear.

In 2019, when a regional alliance in Uttar Pradesh collapsed, one of its young leaders told me, "We didn't lose seats, we lost screen time." He wasn't wrong. Visibility determines legitimacy. In the twenty-four-hour news cycle, the vanquished fade within minutes. A party's office that once buzzed with supporters becomes silent overnight, littered with half-deflated balloons and unpaid volunteers. The republic's attention span measures respect by decibels.

The fear of irrelevance breeds denial. After nearly every state election, leaders who lose issue identical statements: *"We respect the people's verdict but…."* The "but" carries everything that democracy tries to teach us to leave behind - bitterness, conspiracy, self-pity. In 2024, when a chief minister in the north-east resigned after a narrow loss, his supporters blocked highways demanding a recount. "We can't accept that we lost by one percent," a protestor said. But democracy's arithmetic, unlike its morality, has no empathy.

The refusal to lose gracefully seeps beyond politics. In cricket, social media now divides players into patriots and failures overnight. When India lost the 2023 World Cup final, anonymous users flooded the captain's account with abuse. A fan from Kolkata told a reporter, "We don't hate losing; we hate being reminded we are vulnerable." That sentence explains far more than sports. It is the emotional blueprint of the Republic of Winners - a nation that confuses self-worth with scoreboard.

Failure once bred introspection. Now it breeds hashtags. In Parliament, opposition benches that should symbolize dissent are dismissed as "anti-growth." A defeated policy is re-introduced with cosmetic edits and marketed as reform. Bureaucrats call this "repackaging loss." One former secretary recalled how a rural-housing scheme scrapped for corruption was relaunched under a new name six months later. "We don't admit mistakes," he said. "We rebrand them."

For ordinary citizens, the culture of infallibility trickles down to everyday life. In corporate offices, employees celebrate "success parties" but avoid post-mortems. In classrooms, toppers are paraded; those who fail are invisible. A teacher in Bhopal's government school told me, "Our students don't fear exams; they fear labels." The psychology of defeat has been replaced by the pathology of shame.

India's spiritual traditions once honoured humility as strength. The *Bhagavad Gita* speaks of equanimity - success and failure as twins. Gandhi turned loss into moral theatre; his fasts were defeats transformed into persuasion. But in the age of markets and metrics, humility is mistaken for weakness. A bureaucrat who admits error risks transfer; a minister who apologizes risks headlines. So they persist in the fiction of perpetual success.

Digital politics magnifies this illusion. Algorithms reward certainty. On Twitter or WhatsApp, every argument must end with triumph - no nuance, no retreat. "If you concede even one point, they call you compromised," said a young activist from Bengaluru. Debate, once the heartbeat of democracy, now feels like gladiator combat. The loser bleeds like instead of learning.

Yet defeat remains democracy's hidden teacher. It humbles ambition and expands imagination. When a farmer's movement forced the repeal of farm laws in 2021, victory arrived only after a year of hardship. But leaders of the movement insisted, "We also lost - our youth, our time, our illusions." Their honesty made the triumph credible. Loss gives legitimacy to gain.

In contrast, the arrogance of victory breeds decay. After the Emergency, the opposition alliance that replaced Indira Gandhi splintered within two years, undone by ego. The inability to lose within victory is as fatal as the inability to lose at all. "We thought freedom meant we'd never fail again," said a surviving Janata Party veteran. "We forgot that democracy is a continuous correction."

Psychologists call it "defeat anxiety," a trait nations share with individuals. It manifests in denial, aggression, or blame. In India, it manifests in the politics of humiliation. Campaigns rely on derision - *pappu*, *chor*, *anti-national*. Every election becomes an exorcism of empathy. When words like "traitor" or "tukde-tukde" replace reason, losing becomes a moral crime.

But scattered across the country are citizens who practice a quieter wisdom. In Nagaland's village councils, when a proposal fails to pass, elders share tea before adjourning. "We end every meeting in agreement-that we disagreed," laughs an elder from Tuensang. The ritual matters more than the result. It keeps conversation sacred.

After the 2024 general election, a candidate from Tamil Nadu who lost by thirty thousand votes visited his constituency with sweets. "I wanted to thank them for listening," he said. His gesture drew mild amusement but deep respect. The local paper called it *a defeat worth remembering.* Such acts of grace are rare but contagious. They remind people that politics, at its best, is public character.

The real defeat that threatens India is emotional - the loss of tolerance for loss. Nations grow not when they win wars or elections but when they learn to live with disappointment without turning it into hate. Germany after the Second World War, South Africa after apartheid - their moral revolutions began with collective humility. India's freedom movement too was built on learning from failed satyagrahas. Each arrest, each defeat, deepened the discipline of democracy.

In 2025, as India turns seventy-eight, the republic faces a paradox: it knows how to celebrate victories but not how to process failures. The media crowns winners by evening; bureaucracies decorate themselves with "100 percent achievement." But somewhere in that noise, democracy's melody - the right to err, to pause, to reflect-fades.

One night in Lucknow, after the 2022 civic polls, I met an independent candidate who had secured only 127 votes. His poster still fluttered on a lamppost. "I knew I'd lose," he said, "but I wanted my children to see that trying matters." He packed his loudspeaker, smiled, and added, "Maybe next time I'll get 200." That small arithmetic of hope is democracy's hidden pulse - the courage to fail publicly and still return to the ballot.

When a nation learns to respect its losers, it redeems its winners too. For victory without empathy is conquest, and defeat without dignity is despair. Between those two extremes lies the true republic - imperfect, self-correcting, human.

Chapter – 8
The Vanishing Voter

The silence of participation and the fatigue of citizenship.

At dawn on election day in Mumbai's Andheri East, a polling officer yawns behind a table stacked with voter slips. The street outside is still asleep. By evening, barely 48 percent of the constituency will vote. Two hundred kilometers away, in Maharashtra's Gadchiroli district - a Naxal-affected region - turnout crosses 75 percent despite threats and a two-hour walk to the booth. The paradox defines modern India: those with the least to gain vote the most; those with the most to lose stay home.

Participation is the heartbeat of democracy, but India's pulse beats unevenly. In the first general election of 1952, voter turnout was 45 percent - remarkable for a country still learning literacy. Seven decades later, the figure hovers around 67 percent nationally, yet hides deeper apathy. Urban citizens, empowered by information and infrastructure, increasingly abstain. “Why should I vote? Nothing changes,” says a software engineer sipping coffee in Bengaluru’s Indiranagar. In his gated world, governance is an app, not a conversation.

The vanishing voter is not lazy; he is alienated. Democracy promised voice, but delivered noise. Campaigns have become bombardments - calls, messages, hoardings, hashtags. By the time voting day arrives, fatigue sets in. In Delhi’s 2024 municipal polls, one polling booth reported only 39 percent turnout. “People are tired of choosing between slogans,” said a presiding officer. “They don’t see themselves in the system.”

Rural India still votes in large numbers, but out of compulsion rather than conviction. In Bundelkhand, an old farmer confided, “They’ll cut our ration if we don’t.” In another village, a woman voter whispered that her husband told her whom to choose because “the party built our borewell.” The line between loyalty and fear is thinner than ever. Democracy survives on faith, but faith has been replaced by transaction.

For the urban elite, apathy is the new badge of privilege. Election day is a long weekend, not a civic ritual. In 2024, Goa’s beaches were crowded even as polling stations were empty. “We’re registered in Delhi,” said a tourist sipping beer. “Anyway, one vote doesn’t matter.”

That sentence - casual, self-assured - is democracy's quiet obituary. When participation becomes optional for the comfortable, accountability disappears for everyone else.

The machinery of elections has never been more efficient. Booths are digital, queues shorter, ink indelible. Yet the emotional infrastructure - trust, curiosity, dialogue - is collapsing. "We run the world's biggest election, but not the smallest conversation," said a retired Election Commission official. The commission itself, once revered for impartiality, now faces accusations of bias. Its silence on hate speeches and delayed responses to complaints erode the moral authority that once drew citizens to the booth.

Young voters, instead of energizing democracy, are withdrawing into cynicism. In Pune's colleges, students debate politics on Instagram stories but skip voting. A survey by CSDS-Lokniti in 2023 found that fewer than 40 percent of first-time voters had full confidence in the electoral process. "Everyone is corrupt," said a 19-year-old commerce student. "Better to focus on my career." The new nationalism thrives on hashtags, not ballots.

Technology was meant to fix participation but often deepens disengagement. The Election Commission's "My Vote My Right" app boasts 10 million downloads but few active users. Online registration portals malfunction, and awareness drives end with selfies. "Democracy has become performative," said an activist from Hyderabad. "People want to be seen supporting it, not doing it." Digital citizenship without civic substance is just branding.

Meanwhile, those who persist in faith face growing disillusionment. In Assam, displaced citizens living in flood relief camps discovered their names missing from the electoral rolls. In Jammu & Kashmir, redrawn constituencies after the abrogation of Article 370 left many voters confused about representation. "They took away our state, then asked us to trust their vote," said a shopkeeper in Srinagar. His words echo through the hollow architecture of consent.

The cost of participation is also emotional. In Bengal's 2021 polls, voters endured violence and intimidation; yet turnout was record-high. "We vote because we're scared not to," one woman told reporters. Democracy survives through endurance rather than enthusiasm. The republic counts ballots but not bruises.

The media amplifies the spectacle but not the silence. Election-day coverage resembles a cricket match — percentages, mood boards, drone shots of queues. The missing story is the absent voter. Nobody interviews those who stay home. A sociologist in Delhi University calls it "the politics of disappearance." When absence itself becomes invisible, the republic loses its mirror.

Civic education, once embedded in schools, has withered. The National Curriculum once taught children to simulate elections in classrooms. Today, many schools skip civics to focus on coding or competitive exams. "They know more about Elon Musk than Ambedkar," laments a teacher in Lucknow. Citizenship has become a forgotten subject in the curriculum of aspiration.

But across the country, experiments in re-engagement offer quiet hope. In Kerala's Kudumbashree collectives, women discuss local issues before voting, often challenging their husbands' choices. In Meghalaya, church groups conduct voter-awareness drives that connect political participation with moral duty. In rural Odisha, Palli Sabhas debate budget allocations and rank candidates on integrity. These grassroots efforts remind the nation that democracy's energy flows upward, not downward.

The Election Commission's own innovations occasionally spark renewal. The "Model Polling Station" in Madhya Pradesh's Jhabua district, staffed entirely by tribal women, became a symbol of pride in 2023. "Earlier, men told us how to vote; now we run the booth," said the presiding officer. When representation becomes ownership, abstention fades.

Yet structural fatigue remains. A middle-aged voter in Gurugram summed it up: "We have the freedom to vote but not the faith it will matter." Faith erodes slowly, one ignored petition at a time, one unpunished scam, one broken road that never makes it to the budget. When government becomes spectacle, voting becomes ritual. And rituals, when repeated without belief, become empty gestures.

Sociologists describe this phase as "post-participatory democracy" - a system where legitimacy flows from turnout statistics, not genuine involvement.

Governments quote numbers: *highest turnout ever!* But participation without empowerment is theatre. As one tribal elder in Bastar put it, “They take our vote and our silence together.”

Still, democracy’s heart keeps beating in unexpected places. In the remote Ziro Valley of Arunachal Pradesh, villagers paint their fingers with ink before dawn, turning voting into celebration. “This is our festival,” said an 80-year-old woman proudly showing her wrinkled thumb. In her simple act lies the republic’s oldest promise: that the powerless, too, can speak.

India’s challenge is not voter turnout but voter trust. The republic must relearn how to listen between elections - in classrooms, ward offices, and neighborhood meetings. Democracy cannot be delivered every five years; it must be practiced daily.

As polling ends and cameras pack up, the presiding officer in Andheri East locks the EVM and sighs. “We had more volunteers than voters,” she says. Her voice, tired but steady, echoes the quiet crisis of our times: participation without presence.

When citizens retreat into spectators, power fills the void. But the booth still waits - small, unassuming, eternal. It doesn’t demand faith; it offers it. Every voter who returns to that room, even reluctantly, keeps the republic alive one fingerprint at a time.

Chapter – 9
The Great Exclusion: Democracy without Dissent

When disagreement is treated as betrayal.

In January 2020, a winter fog hung over Delhi's Shaheen Bagh. Beneath makeshift tents, hundreds of women sat wrapped in shawls, holding the tricolor. Their placards were handwritten, their slogans steady but soft. "We are the Constitution," one banner read. Around them, police vans idled. News cameras arrived, then left. For a few months, that small stretch of road became India's moral parliament - until the pandemic and bulldozers ended it. The tents were gone, but the silence that followed stayed. It wasn't just a protest that disappeared; it was the vocabulary of dissent itself.

The promise of Indian democracy was not just the right to speak, but the right to disagree without fear. Today, disagreement is treated as disloyalty. Sedition, defamation, and anti-terror laws - colonial relics - are now wielded with digital precision. Between 2014 and 2023, more than 13,000 Indians were charged under the Unlawful Activities (Prevention) Act, many for words rather than weapons. “I’m not a terrorist,” said a student activist from Aligarh Muslim University, “but I’m treated like one because I held a placard.” His trial, like hundreds of others, drags on quietly in lower courts - justice delayed into deterrence.

The republic’s original sin, perhaps, was to confuse uniformity with unity. In recent years, exclusion has worn many faces: the migrant worker stranded on a highway, the farmer fenced out of markets, the journalist locked out of press conferences, the Muslim excluded from citizenship by document, the Dalit from dignity by birth. “Democracy,” said Ambedkar, “is not merely a form of government. It is primarily a mode of associated living.” That association is now fractured.

During the migrant crisis of 2020, millions walked home as cities turned hostile. The state watched, sometimes distributed food, sometimes denied existence. “We were invisible before,” said a worker from Bihar, “but at least we could earn. Now we are invisible and unemployed.” The great exclusion was not just economic - it was existential. The republic had lost the capacity to see its own poor.

Digital India has deepened the divide. Welfare delivery through Aadhaar and direct benefit transfers has improved efficiency but eroded empathy. A tribal widow in Jharkhand starved to death in 2019 after her biometric card failed three times. Her name, Santoshi Kumari, appeared in government dashboards as "inactive beneficiary." Bureaucratic exclusion has become data-driven - clean spreadsheets, invisible suffering. "They call it digital inclusion," said a local activist, "but it excludes those without fingerprints."

Cultural exclusion follows. In textbooks revised in 2023, chapters on Mughal emperors vanished. In television debates, the word "liberal" became an insult. Literature festivals, once spaces for debate, now self-censor. "We don't reject ideas anymore," said a publisher. "We just don't publish them." Even history has been edited to fit ideology. The plural India of the classroom is shrinking into a single story.

The consequences ripple through everyday life. A poet in Lucknow stopped reading his verses in public because local organisers feared protests. A schoolteacher in Gujarat was suspended for showing a film on constitutional values. "I didn't teach politics," she said. "I taught civics." In the Republic of Winners, only one truth may prevail - and it must be shouted, not reasoned.

Exclusion also hides in language. Political slogans claim inclusivity - *Sabka Saath, Sabka Vikas* - yet the rhetoric of "us" and "them" governs the subtext. When "urban Naxal" became a convenient label, dissenting academics and lawyers were painted as traitors. "We used to fear jail," said a rights lawyer from Nagpur, "now we fear irrelevance." The punishment for dissent today is not always arrest; often it is erasure - the quiet cancellation of a voice.

The economy mirrors the same logic. Small businesses, informal laborers, and self-help groups - the very engines of inclusive growth - face policy shocks that privilege corporate giants. When farm laws were passed without consultation in 2020, protestors said, "You made laws for us without us." Their year-long agitation forced repeal, but not reform of the mindset that equates governance with control.

At the margins, resistance continues. In Bastar, tribal women patrol forests to prevent illegal logging, asserting rights under the Forest Rights Act. In Tamil Nadu, fisher folk form climate cooperatives to protect their coasts. In Delhi, a collective of domestic workers started a union during the pandemic. "We realized no one was speaking for us," said their leader. "So we spoke for ourselves." These are small republics within the larger one - still messy, still alive.

Exclusion has also moved online. Social media, once hailed as the democratizer of voice, now amplifies exclusion through algorithms. Hate trends faster than hope. Minority users face coordinated trolling; women journalists receive rape threats disguised as memes. The new public square is less a conversation than a colosseum. "They tell me to log off if I can't handle abuse," says a young reporter. "But this is where the stories are - who gets to stay online is the new privilege."

Even institutions meant to protect inclusion have faltered. The National Human Rights Commission's reports gather dust. Universities that once incubated dissent now police it. The judiciary, increasingly deferential to executive power, delays hearings on constitutional challenges for years. "We used to say the Constitution will save us," remarked a law student in Bengaluru. "Now we must save the Constitution."

Yet exclusion cannot extinguish imagination. Across the country, citizens keep rebuilding small democracies - mohalla committees mediating disputes, farmers' cooperatives running markets, women's groups rewriting Panchayat agendas. These acts of inclusion are quiet, almost invisible, but they sustain the republic's moral oxygen. "We don't need permission to participate," said a tribal elder in Odisha. "We were here before the government."

The story of Indian democracy has always oscillated between belonging and banishment. In 1947, independence promised inclusion; Partition punished it. In 1975, Emergency suspended it; in 1977, voters restored it. Each cycle teaches the same lesson: power centralizes, people decentralize. The question is not whether exclusion will end, but whether empathy will outlast exhaustion.

At a tea stall in Varanasi, a rickshaw puller summed it up better than any manifesto. "Everyone talks about New India," he said. "But where is Old India - the one where we could argue and still drink tea together?" His question lingers - not nostalgic, but necessary. For democracy is not defined by who rules, but by who belongs.

If India must remain a republic of winners, it must first remember those left outside the celebration. Inclusion is not charity; it is survival. And the measure of a mature nation is not how loudly it applauds its victories, but how gently it listens to its silences.

Chapter – 10
Reimagining Representation

Democracy was never meant to be a mirror of power, but a window to the unheard.

In a small village near Dantewada, the Gram Sabha meets under a mahua tree. The agenda: whether to allow a mining lease on nearby hills. A frail woman named Laxmi Bai raises her hand. “These trees feed us,” she says quietly. The government file will later record this as “public consultation completed.” But no one in the capital will hear her voice. Representation in India too often means being mentioned, not being heard.

Democracy was never meant to be a mirror of power - it was meant to be a window to the unheard. Yet over the decades, that window has clouded. India’s constitutional imagination began with the promise that every citizen, regardless of caste, gender, or wealth, could shape the state. The architecture worked beautifully on paper: elections, panchayats, reservations, parliament. But as politics professionalized, the citizen became a spectator.

Representation turned into arithmetic - of caste coalitions, not conscience. In Uttar Pradesh, candidates are selected by “social engineers” who calculate community blocs. In Haryana, khap leaders negotiate tickets as if auctioning contracts. “We don’t need ideology,” one party strategist told me in 2024, “we need distribution.” The voter is no longer a moral agent; she is a demographic variable.

Women’s representation, celebrated through the long-awaited Women’s Reservation Bill of 2023, reveals another paradox. It promises 33 percent of seats for women, but only after a census and delimitation that may take years. “We are always represented in future tense,” quipped a sarpanch from Rajasthan. In practice, many elected women remain proxies for husbands or fathers. “They call me ‘Madam Pradhan,’” said one, “but they still whisper instructions to my husband.” True representation begins not with law but with listening.

The problem deepens in cities. Urban governance - the space where daily life happens - remains the least representative. In Bengaluru or Mumbai, residents rarely know their ward councilor’s name. “Our MP tweets, but our drain overflows,” sighed a civic volunteer. India’s smart-city programs built sensors and apps, but not accountability. Citizens can now click to complain, but seldom to decide.

Parliament itself mirrors the imbalance. The 18th Lok Sabha, elected in 2024, is the wealthiest in history - over 85 percent of its members are crorepatis. Their average age: 55. Their average declared assets: ₹17 crore. The house of the people has become the house of privilege. "Representation is now aspirational," joked a first-time MP. "Everyone wants to join politics the way people want to join startups." But startups at least publish results; parties rarely publish audits.

The mechanics of political funding reinforce this elitism. Even after the Supreme Court scrapped the Electoral Bonds Scheme in 2024, anonymous money continues through shell NGOs and "research grants." Candidates must invest crores to contest; ordinary citizens can only clap from the sidelines. A dalit activist in Bihar described it sharply: "Our democracy is like a wedding hall - you can enter only if you can pay for the invitation card."

Yet India also hosts quiet experiments that expand the meaning of representation. In Kerala, participatory budgeting allows citizens to decide portions of the local development fund. In Nagaland, customary village councils co-govern with elected bodies. In Mumbai's bastis, collectives of domestic workers and migrants have started "people's assemblies" to review ward budgets. "We don't wait for politicians to remember us," said a domestic worker named Rekha. "We remind them."

Digital participation, too, shows glimmers of promise. In 2023, Karnataka's "Janaspandana" portal allowed citizens to track departmental responses in real time.

Though the interface still favours the literate, it hints at a future where accountability is horizontal, not hierarchical. The danger, of course, is that technology can become another filter - efficient but exclusionary. "Democracy cannot be downloaded," warned an election scholar. "It must still be lived."

The media, once the loudspeaker of representation, has drifted into distortion. Marginalized voices appear only as victims or villains. When farmers protested outside Delhi, anchors framed it as traffic disruption, not democratic dialogue. "We are citizens when we pay taxes," said a protester, "but agitators when we ask questions." True representation would mean showing the protester as policymaker, not nuisance.

The judiciary occasionally restores that ideal. In 2023, when the Supreme Court affirmed the right of forest dwellers to appeal eviction, it revived the spirit of constitutional empathy. Yet even courts risk elitism: hearings streamed online but in English, schedules opaque, access costly. "Justice is televised but not reachable," remarked a law student. Representation without translation is illusion.

Reimagining representation, then, demands three revolutions: of **scale**, **space**, and **spirit**.

- **Scale**, because decision-making must travel downward - from parliament to panchayat to mohalla.
- **Space**, because the physical commons of democracy - libraries, parks, schools - must become venues for deliberation, not mere amenities.

- **Spirit**, because representation is not about speaking for others, but creating conditions where others can speak.

In Madhya Pradesh's tribal belt, a local NGO tried something radical: "rotational representation." Each month, a different community elder attended district meetings to report issues. The process was messy, but revealing. "When people take turns at power," said the facilitator, "they realize how hard listening is." That humility is democracy's missing institution.

Art and culture still carry fragments of genuine voice. Stand-up comedians, independent filmmakers, folk musicians - they fill the gaps left by parliamentarians. In Manipur, young storytellers use puppetry to narrate displacement; in Varanasi, street plays teach voters how to verify candidates. These expressions restore politics as performance of conscience, not of command.

The diaspora adds another layer. Millions of Indians abroad cheer elections online, yet cannot vote easily. Their remittances sustain villages, but their voices are absent from ballots. "We send money home but can't send our opinion," said a nurse in Dubai. A future democracy must bridge that paradox - global citizens with local stakes.

Ultimately, representation is not a number but a relationship. It fails not when people disagree with their leaders, but when they stop believing their leaders will listen. In 2024, during a rural development meeting in Odisha, a young bureaucrat asked villagers to raise hands for or against a project. Only one man stood up -

against. Silence followed. The officer thanked him and recorded the objection. Later, the man said, "I thought I'd be scolded, but he smiled. Maybe we still have democracy."

His words capture the essence of re-imagined representation: a small act of dissent, respected rather than punished.

The future will not be decided by how loudly governments speak, but by how many voices they make room for. India's challenge is not population but participation - to ensure that its billion-plus citizens are counted not just as voters, but as viewpoints.

Because democracy, at its core, is not the art of ruling others; it is the discipline of listening to those we don't resemble.

Chapter – 11
The Ethics of Losing

A nation grows up when it learns to lose without hatred.

In May 2024, as election results trickled in, a senior opposition leader stepped onto a stage in Patna to address a restless crowd. "We fought hard," he began, his voice trembling. "But the people have chosen otherwise." The microphones captured his words, but not the silence that followed. Behind him, party flags drooped. Within an hour, television channels cut away to victory speeches elsewhere. The losers had spoken - briefly, respectfully, and irrelevantly.

India's democracy celebrates victory like a festival, but treats defeat like an infection. Parties vanish for years, not to introspect but to recover from humiliation. Candidates switch sides, alliances dissolve, and critics are silenced as “frustrated.” Losing, once an opportunity for learning, has become a source of shame.

The ethics of losing begin with acknowledgment. When Indira Gandhi conceded in 1977, she restored faith in the system she had tested. In 2004, when Atal Bihari Vajpayee unexpectedly lost despite his popularity, he smiled and said, “The people’s decision is final.” Those gestures carried moral weight because they affirmed something larger than power - the sanctity of consent. But in recent years, defeat has become negotiable. Losing parties allege conspiracies, and even winning ones claim victimhood. “We are still under siege,” declared one ruling-party leader after a landslide win. The language of grievance has replaced grace.

This transformation has consequences beyond politics. It erodes the capacity for humility, a virtue central to any democratic culture. In classrooms, students are taught to win competitions, not to accept feedback. On social media, disagreement is seen as insult. “We have lost the art of losing,” says a psychologist in Delhi. “And that means we’ve lost the art of learning.”

The fear of losing also explains India’s obsession with control. Political parties rarely allow internal dissent. Leadership transitions are postponed indefinitely. “Our party doesn’t retire people,” joked a worker in Lucknow, “it just forgets them.” Bureaucracies mirror the same behavior - no one admits mistakes, reports are rewritten, blame is distributed like ration. “Success has many parents,” goes the saying, “but failure is an orphan.” In India, that orphan is democracy itself.

Consider the corporate world. When the pandemic struck, several start-ups folded. Few admitted mismanagement; most blamed "market conditions." A failed entrepreneur from Bengaluru confessed, "Investors forgive losses, but not humility." This culture of denial mirrors politics - a system that rewards narrative over truth. As a result, losing becomes fatal instead of formative.

The ethics of losing also reveal inequality. When a ruling party loses, it calls it a "temporary setback." When an activist loses, it's criminalized. In 2020, student leaders arrested during protests were denied bail for months. Their "loss" - political, legal, personal - was treated as a warning to others. "They want us to forget we can resist," one of them wrote from prison. "But losing doesn't mean we were wrong." That sentence, simple and defiant, defines the moral frontier of democracy.

History shows that societies mature when they learn to coexist with loss. South Africa's Truth and Reconciliation Commission transformed national guilt into confession. Japan's post-war recovery began with accepting responsibility. India's freedom movement thrived on sacrifice precisely because its leaders understood that moral victories outlive electoral ones. Gandhi's defeats - the failed Non-Cooperation, the Salt March arrests, the broken promises - seeded the nation's conscience more deeply than any triumph.

Today, however, even memory of defeat is sanitized. School textbooks glorify victory; the failures of policy, war, or reform are edited out. The 1962 war with China, the Emergency, the Bhopal gas tragedy - all recede from civic curriculum. "We remember only what flatters us," says a retired history teacher. "Our children will never know that failure built this nation too."

In Parliament, apologies have become extinct. When the 2023 Manipur violence displaced thousands, not a single minister resigned. Compare that to 1956, when Jawaharlal Nehru publicly apologized for police firings in Assam. "We failed our people," he said then. The difference is not of ideology but of integrity. Today's leaders measure ethics by optics. To lose face is considered worse than to lose trust.

And yet, beneath this spectacle of denial, India's moral fabric still holds threads of courage. In village panchayats, losing candidates often attend meetings of their victorious rivals. "We still have to repair the same roads," one joked in Odisha. In civil society, movements reinvent themselves after setbacks. When the RTI campaign faced dilution, activists began training citizens to file local information requests instead of waiting for reform. Losing became adaptation.

Even in sports - India's other national passion - lessons of losing occasionally shine through. After India's heartbreaking loss in the 2023 Cricket World Cup final, captain Rohit Sharma refused to blame luck or opponents. "They played better," he said simply. The humility touched millions more than the victory parades that might have followed. For a brief moment, the nation remembered that pride and grace can coexist.

The greatest danger of never losing is moral stagnation. Without loss, there is no empathy. Winners start believing they are the system. "When I was in power," admitted a former minister, "I stopped answering my phone after 9 PM. When I lost, I realized that's when people need you most." Defeat, he said, "is democracy's way of making us human again."

The ethics of losing are not about resignation, but renewal. They require three disciplines: accepting verdicts without vengeance, learning from error without evasion, and letting others win without envy. These are not political skills; they are civic virtues. In ancient Indian philosophy, *yash* (fame) and *apaya* (loss) were twin teachers - both transient, both necessary. Modern India remembers the first and fears the second.

A story from Kerala captures this wisdom perfectly. During a local election, a schoolteacher contested independently against a dominant party and lost by a wide margin. The next morning, she visited the winner to congratulate him and offered her help in education projects. "Why?" he asked, puzzled. She smiled, "Because children don't care who won." That simple act restored what politics had forgotten - that losing honorably can sometimes serve the public better than winning arrogantly.

Democracy matures not through victories, but through the dignity of its defeats. Nations grow up when they can face failure without hatred, correction without humiliation, and difference without fear. India, with all its noise and nerves, still carries that potential. The ethics of losing may yet save the republic - if we dare to practice them.

Chapter – 12
The Future Republic: Equality after Victory

Freedom gave us independence; equality will give us peace.

On a winter morning in 2047, India will turn one hundred. Schoolchildren will march with flags, drones will light up the sky, and speeches will recall the heroes of 1947. But somewhere, in a quiet village, an old woman may whisper to her granddaughter, "Freedom gave us independence; equality will give us peace." Her words will outlast the fireworks.

The republic was built on a trinity - liberty, equality, fraternity. Liberty we understood instinctively; we fought for it. Fraternity we celebrated in festivals and slogans. But equality - economic, social, emotional - we postponed, assuming growth would deliver it automatically. Instead, growth delivered distance: between cities and villages, between men and women, between those who speak and those who are spoken for.

Every decade since Independence has offered a new promise of inclusion - land reforms in the 1950s, reservations in the 1990s, welfare rights in the 2000s, digital empowerment in the 2010s. Each added a layer, yet the foundation still cracks. In 2024, the richest one percent of Indians held more than 40 percent of national wealth. The bottom half shared less than 10 percent. "We have two Indias now," said a school principal in Jharkhand. "One that logs in, and one that lines up."

The pandemic exposed this divide mercilessly. Migrant laborers walking highways beside billboards of space missions; doctors celebrated as heroes but unpaid for months; online classes where half the students had no phones. "Equality," said a teacher in Bihar, "died of network error." Yet amid despair, acts of compassion quietly re-stitched the social fabric. Neighbors cooked for stranded workers, strangers crowdfunded oxygen, farmers donated grain. When institutions faltered, empathy became infrastructure.

The future republic will depend on whether that empathy can be institutionalized - turned from emotion into policy. It requires rebuilding equality not as charity, but as design. This begins with three urgencies: **equitable opportunity**, **equal dignity**, and **ecological balance**.

Equitable opportunity means more than jobs; it means justice. Education must no longer reproduce privilege. India spends 3 percent of its GDP on education - less than what it spends subsidizing fuel and fertilizers. In a government school in Madhya Pradesh, a girl named Rukmini walks four kilometers daily because her village still lacks a secondary school. “They built a highway,” she says, “but forgot a classroom.” A future republic would measure success not by kilometers of road but by kilometers of imagination widened.

Equal dignity demands confronting caste and gender hierarchies that survive beneath modern glass towers. In 2023, Dalit sanitation workers died cleaning sewers in several cities - an atrocity centuries old. “We use machines for elections,” a social activist remarked, “but not for manholes.” Equality after victory means replacing pity with parity. It is not enough to lift people out of poverty; we must also lift them out of humiliation.

Ecological balance links humanity’s survival with justice itself. Climate change is no longer distant news; it is local grief. In Ladakh, glaciers retreat; in Kerala, floods return yearly; in Delhi, children grow up inhaling smoke. Yet green policies often burden the poor - evicting slum dwellers in the name of beautification, taxing rural fuels in the name of sustainability. The future republic must flip the narrative: sustainability should begin with those who sustain the nation - farmers, fisher folk, forest dwellers. “We are the guardians, not the culprits,” said a tribal elder in Chhattisgarh. True equality will mean giving back land, not just compensations.

The second task is moral: restoring **conversation**. The republic of the future cannot survive on monologues of power. It needs platforms where disagreement is sacred again. Town halls, citizen juries, participatory budgets - these must become democratic rituals. In Kerala's local councils, a citizen can still question a minister without fear; in Meghalaya's church halls, policy and prayer coexist. "Democracy is when the government listens even when we are wrong," said a student in Shillong. Listening is the new justice.

Technology will remain a double-edged sword. Artificial intelligence can predict weather, diagnose diseases, and design policies - but it can also entrench bias. "Algorithms can discriminate faster than humans," warned a data scientist in Bengaluru. The future republic must code compassion into its digital architecture - transparent algorithms, data rights, and digital literacy as a civic duty. Equality in the twenty-first century will depend as much on who controls information as on who owns land.

Economically, India's demographic dividend will soon become a demographic demand: jobs for 10 million youth each year. The private sector cannot meet it alone; the state must reinvent public employment - in green infrastructure, rural healthcare, digital public goods. "We need a Mahatma Gandhi National Innovation Mission," joked a young entrepreneur, "one that pays us to imagine." Equality after victory will not mean distributing leftovers of growth but designing growth itself as a public good.

Culturally, the republic must rediscover empathy in politics. Polarization has exhausted even its victors. Elections fought on hate leave governance starved of trust. A young voter in Hyderabad put it sharply: "We don't need leaders who shout louder; we need leaders who listen longer." In the next republic, success will be measured by patience, not populism.

Faith and reason, often seen as rivals, must again become companions. India's spiritual traditions contain deep egalitarian wisdom: *Vasudhaiva Kutumbakam* - the world is one family. But a family thrives only when all its members eat, speak, and dream equally. The future republic will fail if devotion becomes division. Temples, mosques, and churches should be sanctuaries of service, not stages of supremacy.

Equality also demands new metrics of progress. GDP cannot measure joy, nor can stock indices capture justice. Bhutan's idea of Gross National Happiness may sound idealistic, but India once led the world with moral imagination. Why not measure how many citizens can drink clean water, read freely, or walk unafraid? A republic of winners must redefine winning.

At the heart of the new equality lies gender. Women constitute half the population but only 15 percent of Parliament. Yet from Kashmir to Kanyakumari, they keep the republic breathing - as farmers, teachers, caregivers, entrepreneurs.

During the pandemic, women's self-help groups produced masks and managed community kitchens. In their hands, democracy looked less like ideology and more like nurture. "We don't need power," said a leader from Tamil Nadu's SHG network. "We need respect." Equality after victory will mean replacing paternalism with partnership.

And finally, equality must extend to time itself - between the present and the future. Every tree planted, every river cleaned, every child educated is a contract across generations. "We borrowed the earth from our grandchildren," said a farmer in Sikkim. The republic will be judged not by how much it builds, but by how much it preserves.

As the centenary of freedom approaches, the temptation will be to celebrate achievement. We should - but we must also confess incompletion. India has survived against impossible odds, but survival is not destiny. The next century demands a gentler revolution - not of slogans, but of systems that care. The republic will not be rescued by heroes or hashtags, but by citizens who practice quiet fairness every day.

In a government school in Kerala, children were once asked to draw "India in 2047." One sketch showed a woman farmer, a policeman, a robot, and a tree standing hand in hand under the Ashoka Chakra. The teacher asked, "Why the tree?" The child replied, "Because it gives shade to everyone."

That drawing, more than any manifesto, captures the republic we might still become - one where power protects rather than dominates, and where equality is not a promise after victory but the victory itself.

Epilogue - The Republic Within

The highest civic virtue is not to win, but to lose with grace — keeping hope, humility, and humanity alive.

On Republic Day, the tricolor rises to the sound of drums. Crowds cheer, jets roar, children wave paper flags. Yet, amid the parade's perfection, a small boy on the footpath salutes a flag painted on the pavement. His gesture goes unnoticed, but not unseen. He is the citizen the Constitution imagined - humble, invisible, eternal.

Democracy, we often say, is a system. But systems, like machines, wear out. What survives them are habits - the reflex to listen, to question, to care. India's democracy has endured not because it is flawless, but because its people keep mending it in a thousand quiet ways. A teacher reopening a rural school after floods; a journalist asking one more question despite threats; a bureaucrat delaying retirement to finish a village road; a mother reminding her son to vote. These are not headlines, yet they are the republic's real scaffolding.

The journey of this book - from the winners to the forgotten - is not about cynicism. It is about calibration: the need to re-measure success by empathy rather than applause. Power, left unexamined, always seeks permanence; equality, left unattended, quietly erodes. Democracy survives in the tension between the two. The Republic of Winners may dominate the news cycle, but the Republic of Workers - teachers, farmers, nurses, drivers, street vendors - keeps the nation alive.

Every generation inherits not freedom, but its unfinished work. The founders of India wrote a Constitution meant not to freeze time but to evolve with conscience. When Ambedkar warned that political democracy without social democracy would crumble, he was predicting our present moment. We have learned to conduct elections; we have yet to learn to conduct empathy.

The future of the republic will not be shaped by algorithms or assemblies alone. It will be shaped in homes and hearts - in how parents teach disagreement, how schools teach equality, how temples and mosques teach coexistence. The Constitution cannot compel kindness; it can only invite it. And every citizen who accepts that invitation becomes a founder again.

History reminds us that republics rarely die by coups; they decay by comfort. When citizens stop asking questions because their lives seem stable, power grows roots. The challenge, then, is not to overthrow governments but to outgrow indifference. “Eternal vigilance,” Jefferson said, “is the price of liberty.” In India, that vigilance must now include the vigilance of compassion.

To rebuild democracy, we must first humanize it. Voting is an event; justice is a process. We must move from ballots to belonging, from representation to relationship. The Constitution is not a scripture to be worshipped once a year; it is a conversation to be continued daily. Every protest, every petition, every poem that demands fairness keeps that conversation alive.

In the villages of Odisha, elders end their community meetings with a phrase: *"Sab thik hai, par sab barabar nahin hai."* Everything is fine, but not everything is equal. It is both confession and promise. The republic's work is never finished because equality is not a destination - it is a direction.

The "Republic of Winners" will continue to claim headlines, trophies, and timelines. But beneath that glitter, millions will keep building another India - slower, quieter, kinder. The task is not to destroy one to save the other, but to bridge them: to make power answerable and empathy actionable.

As night falls on Republic Day, the boy who saluted the pavement flag sleeps beside his mother under an overpass. Tomorrow he will sell balloons again, unaware that his small salute was the purest act of citizenship. He does not need permission to belong; the Constitution already belongs to him.

And perhaps that is the final truth: the republic is not a promise waiting in Delhi; it is a pulse that beats wherever someone chooses fairness over fear.